SEARCHING FOR LIGHT

Vickie O'Bryant

© April 5, 2013

CONTENTS

INTRODUCTION

As a patient in the Veteran's Outpatient Clinic in Cincinnati, Ohio I've been treated for Schizophrenia for the past 28 years. I am a born again Christian, a single mother of two wonderful sons. Charlie, my oldest son is 24 years old, married and is an Army Veteran after serving in Germany and Afghanistan. My youngest son, Jonathan is 18 years old and is adopted. I live by myself in an apartment on the east side of Cincinnati.

Throughout my childhood I was afraid of a lot of things including people who put me down. I was told many times I would never amount to anything. One psychologist told my parents I would never make it through high school and never be college material. However, I enjoyed singing and doing artwork. I didn't know that God was the One who put those desires in my heart.

I went through a traumatic nervous breakdown during the year 1985, being hospitalized for almost two months and never once thought I would still be alive to tell about it.

DEDICATION

This book is dedicated to my parents, Virgil Arthur and Gladys O'Bryant and my sister, Jackie Ray who inspired me to write my story.

I especially want to thank my sister, Jackie Ray and my friend, Lyn Cravens for editing my book.

I also thank everyone at Create Space who helped turn my dream of writing this book into a reality. Without God and without each one of you, I couldn't have done it! May God continue to bless each one of you.

1   My Military Days

My story starts out where I joined the Ohio Air National Guard after graduating high school in 1977. I wanted to go to college and study music. I didn't make very good grades in all my major subjects, but I thought I had the talent to get into college. After six weeks of basic training in the Air Force I graduated with my flight. My next assignment was to board a greyhound bus to Keesler Air Force Base, Biloxi, Mississippi and attend technical school. I marched to school at 12:00 noon every day. School lasted about three or four hours a day. After school, I marched back to the barracks, changed into my civilian clothes and went to eat dinner at the dining hall. Later, I would go straight over to the recreational center where I would play the piano for hours on end. A couple of times I went to see a movie on base. I also shopped at the store on base. A few times I went to a dance. Being on my own was a very scary thing. When I was in basic training I hadn't gone away from home in my whole life. I quickly learned how to make my bed right, how to fold my clothes and how to sew name tags on my uniforms. I learned all kinds of things, staying up until 9:00 pm every night. I remember being so tired I'd sleep soundly until 5:00 in the morning when those bright lights came flickering on.

I would get up slowly and put my gym clothes on and report downstairs in formation. I did exercises every morning. Then I would march down to the drill pad with my flight and run laps around there. On the last day of basic training we had to run a mile and a half in less than fifteen minutes. I ran it in twelve minutes and thirty-five seconds. I was so hot and tired, but I made it!

After I graduated from Alley Hall at Keesler AFB I knew a lot about working in the orderly room. I was officially an Administrative Assistant. My career field was all about typing forms and discharge packages, filling out forms and every form had a way the military wanted to have it filled out. Even though the material was relatively easy to learn, I studied very hard. Our class also studied the modern office systems such as the IBM stand-alone, telecommunications and data automation.

I went back home to Columbus, Ohio to live with my parents and sister once again. I was assigned to the 121st Combat Support Group at Rickenbacker Air National Guard Base. Each year I was obligated to a two weeks summer training camp.

One year, I pulled summer camp at Barbers Point in Oahu, Hawaii. During that time I was very scared. I met a girl who was also going there and we shared a room together while we stayed on the Navy Base. At first, on the plane ride over there we hit it off to a good start and I really liked her. It seemed like we became good friends. But after rooming with her she started picking on me. I couldn't believe this was the same person. Well, we were assigned the job of working back in the kitchen and at the service line serving food.

One day I didn't go in to work. I overslept and stayed in bed almost all day. I didn't know if my roommate was ever going to come back to the room. She had been out on a date the night before. She and I both missed work that day.

The very next day both of us got called in on the carpet. Not only did we get yelled at, we were both notified ahead of time we would be leaving Hawaii to return back to Rickenbacker. The officer over us said we were going back and that was final. I was so thrilled at the good news, if I could have leaped out of my boots, I would have. On the other hand my roommate protested loudly in response to the officer's strict orders.

One night my roommate had come back to the room from a date. She was angry with me for some reason. I don't know what it was about, but she said if I was smart I would go down to the airmen's club tonight. I told her I wasn't going. I was reading my Bible, too. Then, she asked me what kind of drugs I had been taking. She was really mad at me for something, I don't know what. Then, I got mad at her. I picked up my Bible and started yelling at her to the top of my lungs. I don't know what got into me at all. Then, softly I told her how sorry I was and extended my hand to her. She just stood there, didn't move and said she didn't want to talk to me.

We had gone down to the beach one day. It was so fun, but I didn't venture out into the water. I was afraid I might run into a shark, or something. I just stayed on the beach and watched everyone else swim in the ocean. I had a guy that followed me all over the place and he came with all of us to the beach. He tried to get me to go into the water, but I just said I wasn't going. He even said he would protect me, I think. We actually did go in, but I quickly got right back out. He was so downhearted.

Anyway, the next day we had to pack up and board our flight to go back to Rickenbacker. It was a 23 hour flight on that KC-135 all the way home. I remember I sat right in front of all of the cases of pineapples. It was too bad I didn't get to take one home with me. I hadn't really planned on getting a pineapple or two. But I was anxious to get back home to my parents.

Going straight to the last few minutes on the plane just before landing at Rickenbacker, a sergeant came over to me and sat down. He introduced himself to me and told me that the guy standing up beside my roommate was a heroin addict. He also said she shouldn't be involved with him. I always have gotten scared when people talked about drugs, because I'd had a very bad experience with marijuana and PCP one time. That sergeant also said that he was a black belt in Karate. After he said that I started thinking that he was going to kill me. I don't know whatever caused me to think that about him. I became strapped with the fear of death. Thinking about all the ways he would kill me, I became completely paranoid.

While we were all getting off the plane I saw that guy go over to a pay telephone and begin making calls to someone. I was so scared of him. I was debating whether to tell someone. I latched onto the arms of one officer and begged for his help. I don't recall who he was, but he did help me. He took me back to his office and calmed me down. He simply told me I was not going to be killed or even harmed for that matter. He let me call my parents who also were startled at my voice on the phone. Both my parents wanted to know how and why I came back so early. I had only been there in Hawaii for a week. They, too, were very skeptical.

The point I want to make is this: You don't have to think the worse about someone, or better yet, misjudge anyone. You also don't have to accept any thoughts that someone is going to hurt you, especially if you have never done anything wrong to anyone. You can pray to God and tell Him everything you are going through. Now I know for sure I don't have to automatically misjudge someone's intentions.

My parents brought me up in a Christian home. They taught me some things about the Bible. But, one of the things that really stand out is that they both taught me to do unto others what I would have them to do unto me. I went to church one morning with my cousin. She was only a year younger than I. Debbie and I were close friends, too. She had spent the night at our family's house before it was time to drive to church. We drove to the Williams Road Free Will Baptist Church. There we met our Uncle Charles and Aunt Judy. I can't recall what the sermon was about that day, but I remember when the choir went up to sing "Just as I Am", I started crying. I felt the weight of the Spirit begin to tug at me to go down front and accept Jesus in my life. I just kept crying. Then my cousin and my aunt said if I wanted to go down to the altar, and receive Jesus in my heart I could. They would pray for me. I told them that I wasn't ready to accept Jesus. They kept telling me all the more what if Jesus came tomorrow and everyone went to heaven that were ready, and I hadn't given my heart to Him yet. What do you think would happen, they told me. I told them that I probably wouldn't make it to heaven. They both said, "Vickie, we will pray for you. You don't have to be afraid." They patiently waited for me to decide. Then all three of us went down to the altar and I knelt and saw a miracle take place. I felt a ton of bricks had fallen off my chest. Suddenly, I was free! It was that dramatic. Everyone in the whole church came to hug me and welcome me into the body of Christ. One person said I would never regret receiving the Lord in my heart today.

In March 1980, I decided to join the Air Force and separate from the Air National Guard. So, in June 1980, I departed for Lowry AFB, Denver, Colorado.

I worked in the orderly room at the 3441st School Squadron. I did the same kind of work I'd done when I was in the Air National Guard. Only this time I was given more responsibility. I typed discharge packages, letters of reprimand, article 15s and even court martial packages. I also did filing. When I joined the regular Air Force I didn't have to go back through basic training, which was a big sigh of relief. I became good friends with my supervisor, Sgt. Danny Herrera. Upon arriving at the base I was very scared and had a certain fear of the people I worked with.

After weeks of going to briefings, I met a nice guy who was a sergeant. His name was Dean. We became close friends and started dating each other for a while. We dated for about a year, but it ended with a very sad ending. Dean was a very talented man. He played the bass and the electric guitar. He was also in a band. He loved all kinds of music, mostly rock, hard rock, rhythm and blues and jazz. He had lots of records. One record I remember he had was, The Scorpions. He said The Scorpions were a German rock band. I liked one of the songs he played from that album which was, "The Men in Black." The bass line in that song was very neat. Dean's job in the Air Force was an instructor in the weapons school. He trained the young airmen how to load bombs aboard all of the fighter aircraft, such as the F-4 Phantom. That one carried all of the bombs.

After I had several blow-ups with Dean, I found out he was only keeping me hanging on. I just couldn't see it. He finally broke up with me and broke my heart. I came into work feeling very sad. I didn't want anyone to see I had been crying, so I wore sunglasses to work. That didn't get it at all with my supervisor. Everyone in the office watched while I did my work. I began muffling under my breath and pouting until Danny decided to take me aside and ask me what was going on. We stepped out into the hall, and I broke out into hard, hard crying. Danny said, "Is it Dean?" I told him Dean had visited me in my dorm room and said he was never going to marry me. He said he knew he wouldn't marry someone like me. Then, I kept staring at the glass doors that lead outside. I was going to run right through them, but instead Danny grabbed me by the arm and said could he take me over to mental health on base and have someone talk with me. I said, yes. So, Danny escorted me over to mental health and I went inside and talked with a counselor. Danny told me not to kill myself, because I am so talented. I could sing and draw. And I was a pretty girl, too, with pretty blue eyes. Danny said, "Vickie, you don't have to settle for Dean. You can have just about anybody you want." I really thought Danny was just trying to keep me from hurting myself. I hadn't really believed him.

2 Joining the Mormon Church

When I came back to work my commander talked to me about what had happened. He was a Mormon and he asked me if I knew God. And I told him I did and that I was a Baptist. Lt. Jasmer offered me a book of Mormon to read, and I read some of it. Then, a few more days later he invited me to his house along with Danny. Danny wanted to join the Mormon Church, and I was investigating it. After we sat in the living room talking about it, my commander said, "Vickie, do you know what hell is like?" I said, "It is like fire and brimstone." Then, he said, "No, it is not. What hell is really like is that you are standing outside of a beautiful home. Everyone in your family are inside the house having fun, but you go up to the window and they don't see you. And it is dark out there. That is what hell is like. Then, Lt. Jasmer related to me that now that I know the truth about the Mormon Church, I had to make a decision to join it or not to join it. I said, "I'll think about it some more and let you know later on." He said, "Vickie, if you don't join, then you won't go to heaven now that you have been told the whole truth." As I pondered all of what he said in my heart, I left discouraged and got into my car. I started crying and asking God, "God, why would you send me to hell just because I didn't join this

Mormon Church?" So, the next day when I went in to work, I told my commander I wanted to join his Church. I was so afraid of God's judgment.

During the next one and a half years I became very involved in the Mormon Church, the Church of Jesus Christ of Latter Day Saints. I went to the Singles Ward in Denver, Colorado. It was a church service that was supposed to be for singles. The church had lots of fun activities as well as Sunday school. For the ladies, we went to a group after church and Sunday school that was called, Relief Society. Then, on Monday nights we went to a Family Home Evening group which got together with men and women. We studied the Bible and the Book of Mormon.

The Mormon Church also conducted activities such as dances and parties. I really enjoyed going to those dances and dancing with the different single guys. I found out that the dances and the parties were designed to bring singles together so they could get married and have big families. I loved going to the Singles Ward and all those church activities, because I felt as though I really fit in. I also thought I was very religious and righteous. But, later on I found out that this was the wrong church for me to be a part of. It all seemed to be a wonderful place to worship God. But, as I recall, the worship service didn't have an altar call. They talked about Jesus. But the one they really worshiped most of all was

Joseph Smith. They said that they believed the Bible to be the true Word of God as far as it was translated correctly and insinuating that the Bible was not all true.

In the back of my mind I wanted to believe in the Mormon religion. But, it was just that, a religion. I remember I had a crush on a guy in that church that was also in the Air Force. I would see him a lot at the dining hall on base. He actually didn't work on Lowry AFB. He worked on Buckley Air National Guard Base as a computer operator. He was tall, medium built, had black hair and brown eyes. So, he was very handsome to say the least. One time he came over to my dorm room and knocked at my door. He introduced himself as Steve. Then he asked if he could come inside and told me he was my Bible Study teacher. I was thrilled and let him in. Later, after we talked a while about the Mormon Church, he asked me if I wanted to get some ice cream with him. I said, "Yes!" I thought this was a date. Much to my surprise it was a tease. When we went inside to sit down and order, at first he sat across the table from me. Then, he got up and moved to sit right beside me. He said, "They thought we were sweethearts, didn't they?" After laughing at that and enjoying some good ice cream I quickly became infatuated with him. After leaving Swenson's Ice Cream Parlor, he asked me if I'd like to go with him to the mountains.

I said, "Oh yeah, I sure would love to go!" We got into his car and he drove downtown to Denver, then past Denver and headed toward the mountains. It was late evening when we got there as we traveled over Lookout Mountain. The winding curves and uphill climb was pretty scary. At one point he stopped and backed his car up almost going over the side of the road not to mention over a sheer cliff. He said, "Oh, Vickie, we're not going to make it, ye-ha, ye-ha!" I thought for sure we were going to go right over the side of the mountain. When we left the mountains, the more I thought about this, the more I wanted to tell someone in the church. After I did tell someone at church, they said don't have any more to do with him. Be careful with him. My friends told me not to stop going to church on account of that bad incident with Steve. So, I continued to go to the Mormon Church. And even though I had a bad episode with Steve I was still infatuated with him and still longed to be his girlfriend.

3 A Change for the Better

One day while at work I started writing down some things for the church newsletter. I was given the opportunity to be writer for the church. I called that guy I loved so well named Steve that I had a crush on so much, and asked him if I could write about him in our church newsletter. Right away, after I asked him that, he said, "Vickie, I'd appreciate it if you did not write about me in your newsletter."

I asked him, "Why not?" I probed him to tell me. Then he said, "I've been excommunicated." I asked him why he got excommunicated. And his reply was, "I have found out that the Mormon Church is a cult." He said it was not the true church. I was so appalled at his heartfelt words that I started asking him more questions which led up to my desire to get out of the Mormon Church, too. As I look back over this, I truly believe God used Steve as an instrument to lead me out of the cult of Mormonism. Right after speaking with him about all of this, I wanted to run down the hall and visit my Pentecostal girlfriend, Susan. I came into her office and began telling her, "Susan, I found out that the Mormon Church is a cult." We both stood there and cried. She said, "Vickie, I prayed to God that He would tell you the truth. And He did!"

"Susan," I said. "I'm glad you did!"

Susan asked me if I wanted to go to her church that night. The church she attended was called Happy Church where Marilyn Hickey evangelized. That night I went there with Susan. We walked inside of a Sunday school classroom where two women were doing some paperwork. There in that room Susan and the other two women talked to me about what it means to be delivered. They began by putting their hands on my shoulders and praying aloud. They prayed in unknown tongues, too. Suddenly, I felt free and so happy. I actually felt the angels rejoicing in heaven. When they were praying over me speaking in tongues, I started speaking in tongues as well. I started singing in tongues. I told them that I wasn't afraid of anything anymore. I was so, so happy and just free like a bird that finally gotten let out of her cage.

One Sunday morning I decided to go to the church on base. There were lots of people in that church service, both civilians and military. In that particular church service the chaplain told us whoever wanted to stand up and give a testimony was encouraged to do so. So, I stood up with some of the others who were giving their testimony, and I gave mine. I gave God the glory for delivering me out of the cult of Mormonism. After the worship service I left and went outside to get into my car and go back to my room in the dormitory. A woman came over to me just before I got in my car, and she introduced herself to me as Sylvia. She told me that she really enjoyed my testimony and asked if I'd like to attend her Bible Study. Right away I said, "Yes." And I told her my whole testimony going through every little detail possible. I felt the presence of the Lord. She asked for my phone number at work and at home. Then she said she would call me and let me know when she could pick me up to bring me over to her house for Bible Study. She said she taught the Bible Study, too.

After attending her Bible Study group I'd grown to know her and her family personally as well as some of the others who attended it. Once we picked up a lady, named Nancy. It wasn't long before I found out that she was living with Sylvia's oldest son, Burt. Sometimes we would hold the Bible Study at Burt and Nancy's apartment. Nancy was beautiful. She had blond hair and was fair skinned. Her face looked as perfect as a doll.

Sylvia became my mentor as she mentored the others in the group. When I first came to her group she was teaching in Matthew's gospel at about the 13th chapter. I remember it well, because we went around the room and each of us had a couple of scriptures to say and explain about. When it came my turn I said my two verses, but I had a hard time explaining what I'd read. I was afraid to talk in front of everyone there and I stumbled over my words and had a hard time speaking. I have had this same problem since childhood.

I had lots of trials and tribulations I'd gone through getting overwhelmed and crying about them. But Sylvia encouraged me to keep walking in my journey with the Lord. Often, I would have thoughts that the devil put in my mind. Thoughts like: nobody loves me or I'm not really saved and on my way to heaven. Lots of times I'd had depression. And I was seeing a psychiatrist on base at mental health. I told all of this to Sylvia. I told her that I had a hard time in school when I was growing up.

4 A New Home in Denver

One day when I went in to work my supervisor met me and said he'd like to talk with me in the commander's office. Right away I thought I had been in trouble. I went in and sat down quietly. My commander told me right then that my career focus had changed. I was going to have to be discharged soon under the Early Separation Program. I wasn't prepared for leaving the Air Force so soon. I struggled with the dilemma of whether or not to go home to Ohio after being discharged. The friends I had in the Bible Study were very important to me. It seemed as though this became a turning point in my life. On August 1, 1983 I was honorably discharged from the Air Force.

Before leaving the Air Force, my friend Susan had located a boarding house in the downtown Denver area. She went down to look at the place and she told me about it. It was an old Victorian mansion and it had three floors. I was excited about seeing it, so Susan and I drove there so I could talk to the people about renting a sleeping room. After looking it over, I decided this was where I wanted to stay when I left the Air Force. It was called the Heart of Denver. It was a big place. It had a huge living room, including a studio grand piano, and a large kitchen and dining area. The room I lived in was on the third floor in the attic.

Before I could move in I had to make sure I had enough money for the first month's rent. So, I waited until I received my last paycheck. I had to go to a lot of different places on the base in order to fulfill my separation. When I received my last check I went to cash it on base and also withdraw everything I had in my savings account. I was then able to go to the Heart of Denver boarding house to pay my first month's rent. I had a car at that time. It was a 1977 Chrysler, New Yorker. I had a lot of help from a couple of friends who carried all of my belongings out of my dorm room on base. We loaded everything in my car. It took 2 or 3 trips to get everything in my new bedroom apartment.

I liked it there, because I could get breakfast and dinner at no charge. It was included in the rent. I also liked to play the piano and played it often. It was also pretty much close to a lot of businesses downtown, and I began looking for work every day of the week, Monday through Friday. I rested on the weekends, and went to Bible Study and church. Sometimes, through the week Sylvia would come over and take me to look for work, or to job interviews. She'd also given me money now and then so I could buy my personal care items and toiletries.

Meanwhile, both my parents said they wanted me to come home. They told me that it just wasn't right for me not to come home to my family and live. I tried telling them I was an adult, and I no longer needed to live with them. Then, later they decided to come out there in their truck to try to get me packed up, and talked me into going back home with them to Ohio. They also brought Jackie, my only sister with them. Jackie had her little boy and girl, (Jason and Amanda) stay with the babysitter in Ohio while they came out there.

When they arrived, I brought them into the Heart of Denver and showed them around the place and took them upstairs to see my bedroom apartment. They really thought it was nice. We then went out to a restaurant and then to a motel. They told me I needed to come back home with them. As the night drew nearer we talked about going back home to Ohio. Mom, Dad and Jackie stayed up with me real late that night trying to talk me into going back home. Time and time again I refused their requests. Then my dad said that I was breaking their hearts. Finally, we all went on to bed, but Jackie and I stayed awake talking into the night.

The next day we went to the unemployment office to check when I would receive my unemployment check. There had been a lot of confusion and I grew very angry and started yelling at my parents out in the parking lot inside the truck.

Then Jackie and our parents decided to get out of the truck. When I calmed down we all drove back to the Heart of Denver, then on to a local restaurant to get something to eat.

I think my family stayed in the motel about 5 or 6 days. When they went on to their motel room I called Sylvia who told me that Nancy (Sylvia's son's girlfriend) wanted to come over to see me, and go out to eat dinner. She said I could just tell my parents that Nancy came over to go to dinner with me, and could she come along to the restaurant with us. Nancy came and we talked about it. Then when my family came to see me I introduced them to Nancy. I said she wanted to take me out to eat. Then I asked my family if Nancy could come with us to a nice restaurant and eat dinner. They said, "Sure your friend can come with us to eat dinner." And out we went to a Chinese restaurant. As we sat at our table we talked about how tasty the food was, and Jackie asked my friend how long she'd known me. She said that she and I had known each other for at least a year. My family wanted to know if Nancy was from Denver. But she told them she was originally from Havre, Montana. Finally, Nancy said she met me at Bible Study. My family looked at Nancy, and then looked at each other, but didn't say too much about it. Nancy went on to say that we have a great time studying the Bible. Nancy asked Jackie if she, too, was from Montana, because she looked very familiar. Jackie looked at Nancy and said, "I was born there." Nancy kept saying that Jackie really looked familiar. But Jackie reassured her that she couldn't possibly have known her, because we left Montana in 1963 when Jackie and I were little girls. Dad said briefly that when we were stationed there in Montana he had taken some night classes from Montana State College in Havre. After we ate our dinner, we left the restaurant and Nancy went back over to see Sylvia and fill her in on everything we'd talked about at the restaurant. My family took me back to my apartment at the boarding house. They asked me more and more if I would give it some more thought about going back home with them. Dad had driven his truck out there, and they could easily put all my belongings in the bed of his truck. I kept telling them I was trying to see if I could get a job at Martin-Marietta Denver Aerospace. I really think my family was afraid I was going to get hurt out there living all by myself. They wanted me to forget about finding a job out there, and just come back home with them.

The next couple of days they decided to leave and go down to visit my Uncle Jerry and Aunt Gail in Colorado Springs. Then I hugged them goodbye, told them not to worry, and reassured them I loved them before they left.

5 Finding Employment

The very next day after my family left I got a call from the employment office at Martin-Marietta. They scheduled me to come in for an interview and I passed the typing test and passed all the other tests I had taken. After careful examination of my tests during the interview they decided they could use me in the back entering information into the computer. I was hired as a data entry clerk. I started out working 40 hours a week. As time went by they asked me if I wanted to work overtime and I definitely agreed to that. I worked there in that place for about 6 months. Then one day I got a job interview from another section of the company. It would be at the engineering building over at the main plant in Littleton. I was hired there at a tool crib doing lots of different things. I made copies of tool drawings for them; I did lots of writing; and I also did some computer work. That was a job I really didn't like as some of the people I worked with got on my nerves. It kept getting worse all the time. They had me work through the week, Monday through Friday. But they also wanted me to come in on Saturday, or Sunday at any given time. I had a very early start each morning. I had to get up at 4:00 am and get ready, eat a few bites of something, and then go out the door to catch 3 different busses to work. It wasn't fun. When they told me to come in Saturday morning at 6:00 am, I was so exhausted I couldn't keep my eyes open, but I tried so hard. Because there were no busses that ran on the weekends to the plant, I managed to get a friend from Bible Study to drive me down to where I worked. He didn't like doing it, because it was 10 miles from his home to mine, then 20 miles further down to the main plant. Then he had to drive back to his house, then come and pick me up later and take me home. I wanted to pay him, but he wouldn't accept any pay. I felt bad about that, but he probably had to do it, since his wife was the one who taught the Bible Study. She might have encouraged him to do it, because he would be a better witness as a Christian. And I continued to depend on them for just about everything.

One day I came in to work late and my supervisor turned me in to the head of the department. He was very mean, bawling me out and treating me as if I was irresponsible. He asked me why I was late and why I couldn't have telephoned ahead of time to let someone know. I explained to him that I had spent the night at a friend's house. She was pregnant and very sick. I also told the manager who was questioning me that I wanted to help her by coming over to her house and comforting her. I further explained to him that I didn't have a way back home to my apartment, and had to spend the night at her house. I tried to find a bus that would take me to work. Unfortunately, I was very late for work today. Then, he said, "I don't care if your friend dies! I want you to come in to work every day and on time every day." He also said to me that he didn't think I should be working there in the tool crib. So, he told me that there was a job opening at another part of the main plant in the Failure Analysis Laboratory. He told me to go over there and meet someone about the job. If they hired me, I would still be working at Martin-Marietta, but if I didn't get that position I would have to look for a job elsewhere. I was upset, but I think I handled it well.

I went on over there to the other building and talked to a man who was in charge of the laboratory. He basically told me about the job and what I would be doing. He said that I would be processing all the failure analysis reports in the Wang computer. Then, he took me back in the lab and showed me around the place. It was after hours and no one was there except for the manager and me. He said if you want to come back tomorrow I can get you started. Evidently he must have liked me enough to hire me right then. I thought that was so nice to still have a job at Martin-Marietta. The next day I went in to the tool crib and told the boss I was hired yesterday at the FA Lab. He said, "What? How did you manage to get the job?" I said, "He must have liked me enough to hire me."

So, that night when I went home I told my friends about getting the new job. I also had a dream that night about the place where I would be working. The dream started out where I was in the lab working, and there was a big Anaconda snake slithering on the floor and coming toward me. Then I saw Jesus and He picked up the snake and wrapped it in heavy duty tin foil. And then Jesus said the snake couldn't hurt me, and I would be safe with Him. I confided in my friend, Sylvia and told her almost all the dreams I'd been having ever since I first met her. She seemed to be very interested in knowing all my dreams, and I wanted to find out what my dreams meant.

Ever since I met Sylvia at the church on Lowry AFB, I had been a regular member at her Bible Study most of the time. Sometimes, our study lasted for hours into the night. But it was fun! Later on, I found out that Sylvia's oldest son, Burt was married to Nancy by common-law. The two of them lived together for approximately 12 years. They had an apartment in Cherry Creek which was a suburb of Denver. Nancy worked as a secretary, and her Burt worked at Martin-Marietta as a computer programmer/analyst. Burt was so funny. He would have us cracking up all the time, and he would say all kinds of funny things. He was like a comedian. Nancy loved music and loved to sing. She had a very beautiful voice and could play the guitar, too. She would share songs with us and one song I remember particularly was, 'Pass It On'. One time, I brought my guitar to the group and played and sang some songs also. I'd sing, 'One Day at A Time', 'This Little Light of Mine', 'Wayfaring Stranger' and a couple of songs I had made up. They all seemed to like the songs Nancy and I played for the group. We would start out praying, open up with testimonies and songs and last of all, we'd go into the lesson. When I started with them we were in Matthew's gospel. I grew so much.

6   The Revelation

One day, I was at Sylvia's house, and I told her about a dream I had about Burt and Nancy and me. The dream was where I had gone over to visit Nancy at her apartment. I told Nancy that I was so happy for her, because I found out that Burt wanted to get married to her. I told her he had an engagement ring to give her. She told me in the dream that she hoped he didn't have a ring to give to her, because she was not going to marry him. Then, I left her there at her apartment, got into my car and drove over to Burt's house in Englewood where he had moved to after moving out. As I drove up into his driveway I could see clearly that there was a big wall surrounding the front of the house and Burt was in there. The wall was high over my head. But, someone in the dream told me I could climb that wall. It took me 3 times to try to climb over and on the 3rd time I went over to the other side and went into his house. Burt was in there in the living room going from one side of the room to the other working on computers. I kept trying to get into a conversation with him, but he said, "Wait a minute Vickie and we'll go out to dinner." That is where this dream ended. After I told the dream to Sylvia she shared with me that Nancy had broken up with her son, and it became a crisis. Burt had gone over to Nancy's apartment to tell her he loved her. She was with a bunch of people outside the apartment, and she had a boyfriend over there and he got mad and all the guys had surrounded him with a baseball bat. Although he was unharmed, Burt had left there upset and broken, because of the way he had been treated by Nancy and threatened by Nancy's new boyfriend. That is where there relationship had ended. It was heart wrenching to just hear about it from his mother. But, Sylvia said one more thing which I wasn't aware of. She said that the dream revealed that I would be the one to break the wall he had between himself and the rest of the world, and I would be the one he would marry. Since she had told me that that day I was convinced that he was the man God had for me to be my husband. I kept having more dreams about Burt. The more dreams I had about Burt, they seemed to coincide with being, or becoming his wife. One time I dreamed he was preaching in a church. Sylvia told me that apparently someone had said that her son had a call on his life to become a pastor. I was really excited about all of this. I really hoped to be Burt's wife. But, I didn't believe my family would ever accept him and his family, because of his race. They were African American. My family didn't believe in marrying outside of the race, because our pastor at the Williams Road Free Will Baptist Church had said it was wrong for anyone to marry someone outside of his race. I knew in my heart I wanted to marry Burt someday, because it very well could have been God's idea. Burt and I talked a few times together, but we never did go out together alone at a restaurant or a movie. I was waiting for that to happen. I just got tired of waiting. Then all these bad things started happening to me. I started going through a lot of trials. Sylvia told me a few times that Burt would ask me out some day and not to worry.

One afternoon after coming back in to work from lunch break, I crept into the office. A co-worker was waiting for me to finish up some paperwork of his. He told me that if I didn't have to take so long at lunch talking to everybody then I'd be finished with his project. I simply told him I was trying to bring somebody to the Lord for salvation and that saving someone's soul was more important than any old job. Then he said, "I think that your Bible Study group is cultic if you should ask me." I got real quiet and said I would do his paperwork for him. I was so frightened I forgot about my job. I became confused and ready to give up and quit my job for good. Or, worse yet, I thought about getting a job somewhere else. I called Sylvia on the phone and told her everything that happened. She told me, "You do have something to be afraid of – it sounds like some of the people there at work are devil worshipers."

I went downhill after that. The Bible tells us not to be afraid of the people who can kill the body, but to be afraid of the One who can kill both the body and the soul – God. Not only did I become afraid, I started worrying and getting impatient and worrying about my circumstances. I started becoming prideful. When I went back to work the next morning I started acting mean toward the others at work and I forgot to use the weapons of warfare which the Bible speaks about in Ephesians 6:10-18. My behavior was going downhill fast. I had a very bad attitude.

One day I walked into the computer room to do some work on the Wang computer. Another co-worker told me that the sky is falling. She and another co-worker both started laughing at me. As I thought about what she just said, it didn't dawn on me that she was only kidding. Instead, I took her seriously and started thinking that I would be taken to a high building and pushed out a window. I didn't run to tell my boss or my supervisor about being scared. I just kept all my feelings inside and wouldn't talk to anyone. Not even my best friend Sylvia. The pain of wondering if I'd be murdered was far greater than any pain I'd ever faced. So, I put on a mask to cover up all of what I was going through. I went back home to the boarding house after work. I stayed in my room and didn't venture out of there the whole night. But that night was so strange. I remember lying in my bed trying to go to sleep. I was crying and then I felt some sudden movements from my lips. I felt like there was a small draft going inside of my mouth and my nose. It really felt strange. Not knowing what this was and being very tired I went on to sleep.

The next morning when I got up to put my clothes on and fix my hair I saw myself in the mirror. I was shocked to see a horrible sight. I looked at my eyes real close and I saw that my eyes were very scary looking. Almost as if I were demon possessed. Then, I went downstairs to get some breakfast. After I had breakfast I decided to go back to my room instead of going in to work that day. While I was walking up the stairs I heard a voice audibly tell me, "Don't be afraid. How would you like to work for me now?" I knew this was the devil speaking to me. After going in my bedroom and locking the door behind me I knelt down on my knees and told the devil out loud to get out of my body.

He started laughing at me. I actually heard him laughing. He said, "Satan cannot get out of you. He is here." I don't know what else I said after that. But, I think I screamed at him at the top of my lungs. I repeatedly said, "In the name of Jesus, you get out of me!" I didn't really know what else to say. I was at my wits end. It seemed as though nothing worked.

The next few hours I got back up out of bed and decided to go down to the VA hospital and tell them I was hearing voices. I thought that the doctors could help me somehow. When I arrived I told them who I was and that I had gotten out of the Air Force in August 1983. I asked them if I could see a doctor so I could get some help for all of what I was going through. The doctor saw me after finding my records. I told that doctor absolutely everything. There was a nurse also in the room with us. I told him that I thought that there were devil worshipers where I worked and where I lived. I told them I was hearing the devil's voice and was extremely scared that someone would kill me. I told them that sometime last year I had a dream that I knew I was going to be married to a Christian man who would preach in a church. I said a lot of things without really thinking about what I was telling the doctor.

He told me it did sound to him like I had a good reason to come down to the hospital today. He said that there really are people who are Satanists here in Denver and to be very careful. He also said that my hearing voices could be that I may have a severe case of psychosis and he offered to let me use the VA hospital for treatment. He said he could call someone and then they would drive me down to another VA facility in another town. He told me that the doctors would make sure that I was taken care of right away. Well, after he said all of that to me, I asked him if I could call a couple of people. Then he told me I should really take a long vacation and go back home to Ohio.

First, I called my mom and told her everything. She seemed worried for me. I told her everything would be all right. Then, I said goodbye and started calling Sylvia. I told Sylvia, too, about all of this. Sylvia began telling me that if I wasn't sure I needed to go to a mental institution then I should not go. She said a lot of things about all the crazy people that are in mental hospitals and that I didn't need to go there with all of the education I had. So, I said, "Ok, I won't go." Then she said, "I'll come down there to the VA hospital and pick you up and take you back to my house. Then, we can talk about it." Much to my surprise, when Sylvia pulled up in the car to get me her daughter, Necie was driving. After she stopped the car, Sylvia got out of the front passenger's seat and had gotten in the back seat. I didn't know what was about to take place.

When I'd gotten in the car in the front seat, Necie started bawling me out. She was literally trying to gloat me into a fight. I kept real quiet and didn't say anything at all. But, I was scared to death that she was going to beat me up. She kept saying things like, "Don't let me down, Vickie!!! You've let a lot of people down, but don't let me down!" She was very mean and was yelling at me and everything. I was so sure that she and her mom were both going to beat me up. I was so hurt by all of the things she said to me. And after all that happened I decided that I would just go on back home to my family in Columbus, Ohio. I'd decided right then that I didn't want to be punished or beaten or hurt any more than I'd already been.

7   Leaving a Good Job Behind

The revelation I had about Burt came to me in 1984. During the spring and summer of 1985 I went through lots of trials, and horrible things were happening to me. I became scared, frightened and worried that my revelation wouldn't come to pass. I started believing the lies of the devil, and he was telling me that I was in danger of the judgment and God was mad at me. I became so scared of everything. I thought some of the women where I lived in the boarding house were witches and planning my death.   I no longer trusted God through any of this. I had been acting as if I was a young teenager, but I was actually 27 years old. I was so sure that God was mad at me. I believed that He was going to use somebody to kill me. Although I was panicked and paranoid I never once let anybody know how I was really feeling deep inside. That was a big mistake. I became so afraid I decided to just leave everything and get out of Denver on a jet airliner. I went outside to the payphone, called my boss and told him I was sick. I said I would go to the hospital, and then be back on Monday morning for work. He said, "Ok Vickie." Then I called my mom and asked her if she was going to be home all day that day. She said she was going to be there all day. Then she said, "What are you going to do today?" I told her I was going to go to work. However, I wanted her to think that even though I had plans of coming back home. I figured that if I came back home to Ohio I would be all right, and I would be with my family even if I was to be killed.

I got my paycheck out of my hand bag, and took only my check and my change purse with me. I went outside and saw a cab driver and flagged him down. I told him to take me to the grocery store so I could get my check cashed and then go to Stapleton Airport. That cab driver acted real funny. He asked me where I was going to and what I was going to do once I got there. I told him that I was going on vacation to Ohio. Then he asked me why I wouldn't want to go to Hawaii or somewhere like that. I kept putting him off, not really wanting to tell him anything. I finally arrived at the airport and much to my surprise all the lines were long and busy. Everyone was standing in long lines trying to buy their ticket and check in their luggage. I got in the shortest line and got right up there and the Airline attendant said I would have to go over to the other line and get my boarding pass. I was very mad and anxious, and very nervous to say the least. When I got up there to buy my ticket to Columbus, Ohio the attendant told me he needed 200 dollars. I laid the money out for him and counted it. Then he took my money and counted it again and said he needed 20 more dollars. I gave him the 20 dollars to get through there so I could get to the gate to board the plane. I hadn't packed a suitcase or brought anything with me out of my apartment. All I wanted to do was go straight home. I had decided to leave Denver, my job, and all my friends out there. I decided not to even say goodbye to anyone. I decided that I wanted to live rather than stay there in Colorado to see if Burt would marry me. I thought if I'd gone back home I'd be all right. What a big lie that turned out to be. As I got off the plane in Port Columbus I went outside to get into a cab. I knew how to get back to my parents' house. I told the cab driver where to go. I wanted him to drop me off at the next house down from my parents' house. I walked up to the house, knocked on the door, and someone came to the door. I told them who I was and asked if I could use their phone to call my mom. He told me to come on in and I could use his phone. After I called Mom on his phone I said, "Mom, this is Vickie. I've come back home, and I'll be over there in a little while." Then she said, "Vickie, did you come back home?" I said, "Yes, I came back home to see everybody." When I walked down the driveway my mom was standing outside waiting for me with arms wide open. But I was still scared even though I had come back home safely.

8   My Hospital Stay

I didn't tell my parents or anyone how I was feeling. But more and more they knew something wasn't right. My family finally decided to take me to the hospital to see a doctor. The doctor told my parents they should admit me to the psychiatric unit. My family was having financial problems at that time. So the doctor told them if they wanted to save some money they would be better off taking me to the VA hospital. It wouldn't cost anything at all, because they both told the doctor I was an Air Force veteran. Evidently, the cost of a hospital stay was very costly and my parents just weren't financially able to pay for my hospital treatment, because they didn't know how long I'd be there.

The next two months I spent in the VA hospital in Chillicothe, Ohio. It was just horrible. I was afraid of everybody and thought the doctors and all the patients were planning my death and that all of them were devil worshipers. I also thought that my parents were not really my real parents. I thought my real parents had been killed and the devil worshipers had gotten together to make themselves look like my family members. I was really very sick. And it was all because I didn't talk to somebody about how I was feeling. I bottled it all up inside, and I didn't want to say anything to anybody for fear that I would be killed.

After a few days of testing, I saw a couple of doctors who asked me lots of questions. Some of the questions they asked me were: Are you hearing voices now? When did the voices start? Are you feeling suicidal? Are you afraid of anyone in particular? Are you getting any messages from the TV or the radio? I told the doctors I was hearing the devil's voice. I told them I was afraid I would be killed. I also told them I was getting messages from the TV and the radio. When my parents came to see the doctors who had seen me they informed them I had had a complete nervous breakdown. It was the worse one they had ever seen. They also told my parents that I had been diagnosed with Paranoia Schizophrenia and they were treating me with antipsychotic medicine.

One day while in the day room in the VA hospital I saw a man walk into the room. He had on a white shirt and a white pair of pants. He seemed to be at peace. He sat down beside me and simply told me that everything was going to be all right. He asked me if I prayed, and I said I did. Then he said keep on praying. You'll be all right. I can't remember ever seeing him again. I think he must have been an angel. I believe in angels. They are all around us, guarding us day and night. But what's more important is that Jesus is with us and He will never leave us. I really thought that God had left me, but I didn't know He was really here with me all along. I have finally come to know the peace and security of the Lord in my life now. But, it has taken me 28 years to know that peace.

When I finally got out of the hospital for good I had done real well on the medicine the doctors had given me. Before I left the nurse told me, "Vickie, you keep taking your medicine and you won't have to come back to the hospital." I said, "All right, I will. I'll do that."

9 Moving to Allentown

My parents and I stayed at our home for what seemed like for 2 more years. My dad worked at Executive Jet Aviation adjacent to Port Columbus. He'd worked there for 11 years after retiring from the United States Air Force in 1975. In 1986 a good friend of his called him on the phone from Allentown, Pennsylvania. He asked my dad if he wanted to come up there and work for him as the avionics manager. My dad decided to go up to visit him at Northeast Jet, Limited, on the other side of Bethlehem Steel. My dad really wanted to work for him so he accepted the job offer.

We packed all our clothes, and kitchen and bathroom items and some of our furniture and were able to move up there. My mom and I decided to join a health spa that was very close to our apartment where we lived. I lost weight, went from 180 pounds to 140 pounds, and I looked nice. I kept working out at the spa with my mom. One day I received a letter in the mail from my high school. It was an invitation to my 10 year high school reunion. I was so excited about that. Especially since I'd lost all that weight, I wanted to go and show off my new figure. I talked Jackie into going with me to the reunion. This was in 1987 and she said that her brother-in-law, Jeff would try to pick me up at the airport. So, when I got dressed that morning I made sure I looked good. I wanted to look nice that day, because Jeff just might be able to get me at the airport. I had seen Jeff before, because when I lived in Columbus, he came to our home and asked if I would like to eat dinner with him at Mark Pi's China Gate. He hadn't asked me out since then. So, I wanted to impress him this time. He did come to get me at the airport, and we hit it off to a good start. He seemed real nice and I began being very talkative to impress him. Before he drove me out to Jackie and Randy's house, (Randy was Jeff's brother) he asked me if I was hungry or thirsty. I said I was thirsty and we drove to a restaurant to get something to drink. It might have been Denney's or something like that. He and I drank iced tea and coffee, and talked for a long time. We must have been there for an hour or so, because we didn't get out to Jackie's until it was in the late afternoon.

I stayed with Jackie for about a week. We went out to lunch and over to Columbus to Eastland Mall and shopped for clothes and other things to wear to the reunion. I also remember that I got these 4 inch high heels that were turquoise. And I bought a beautiful satin turquoise two-piece dress with spaghetti straps under the jacket, flowers embroidered around the tail of the jacket and the hem of the dress, too. Jackie also bought an outfit. When the big day came we went out to the

Groveport Country Club in Groveport, Ohio. They had a big nice buffet dinner and there was dancing, a band and a cash bar. I saw my high school principal, but he did not look the same as I'd seen him in my senior year. Pat Johnson was sitting with us and he recognized Jackie, because he had been the best man at her wedding when she married Roger, her first husband. I saw a lot of my old friends and I talked with many of them. I wanted to get up there and dance. I danced regardless of how bad my feet were feeling. Jackie and I had a wonderful time that night. But it ended and we went home to her house. She and Randy lived about 10 or 15 miles north of Newark. It seemed like it was a long way from Groveport to Newark, then north of Newark out in the country was where Jackie and Randy lived. It just seemed like it was so country-like. She and Randy had cages out in their yard with some rabbits, raccoons and squirrels in them; a huge garden in the front yard; and a big hill in the back of their house where they often retreated to pick blackberries. Randy worked in construction and Jeff also worked construction with him.

They had an old two story house that was back in a hollow. Jason was seven years old at that time, and Amanda was three. They actually lived near Fallsburg and that is where they went to school. I remember one day when I was there Jackie and Randy decided to go down to swim in the creek.

Jeff went with us, too. It was a blast. The next day it seemed like, I had to go back home to Allentown. When I got back home I had a card ready to send to Jeff. It was a card that had a grid on the front of it and on the inside of the card it said the words, "Let's get on with the program!" I wrote a cute little note in there and then mailed it out.

10 My Fiancé

Once when I was talking to Jackie on the phone from Allentown she said Jeff was coming over there every day and talking to her and Randy about weddings, and weddings in a church, and weddings outside, and everything in between. She said he kept talking about weddings! We laughed about it. But, secretly I was hoping he would ask me to marry him.

Things went on from day to day as usual. Dad went to work at Northeast Jet, and Mom and I stayed home or worked out at Spa Lady Fitness. Then, one day Jeff called and I talked to him for a little while. He asked me what I thought about him coming up for a visit. I said, "Yes, you can come on up here to visit us if you want."

He came up and stayed for the weekend. We took him to New York City with us and drove around all over the place. Then we went on a picnic on our way back home, just Mom, Dad and Jeff and me. The next day we went to our favorite Chinese restaurant in Allentown. Jeff spent the night on the couch, and I went to my bedroom. On the last night that he stayed with us, he and I went outside for a walk up the street. He held my hand as we walked. Then we sat down on a picnic table. He looked right at me and said, "What program were you thinking about when you sent the card to me?"

I told him, "I don't know. I was just thinking, maybe......."

He kissed me suddenly and said, "Were you thinking about getting married?"

"Married?" I asked. "Do you want us to get married?"

He said, "Yes, I want to marry you Vickie. Will you marry me?"

I practically jumped out of my skin and said, "Yes, I will. I will."

11 My Wedding and Marriage

     In the evening after we came back in from our walk, we sat down in the living room. Jeff and I were very much excited about all of this. And Mom was smiling at us as if she might have known what he was about to say. So, Jeff asked Dad if he could have my hand in marriage. It was such a happy evening for all of us. Dad came over and shook Jeff's hand and said, "Welcome to our family." That night Jeff had to go on back home to his house in Granville, Ohio. He had to get back in time to go to work the next morning. He called me the next day and asked me when I thought would be a good time to get married. And where would we get married. All the important questions were so exciting to me. He let me pick a date, and I decided on sometime in the fall, in September. I think it was early spring when we had decided we wanted to get married. All I could think about was the wedding. Later on, I went up to stay with Jackie. Jackie took me to pick out the invitations. I stayed with Jackie and Randy for about two months or more. Jeff and Randy went to work every day. Jackie and I went to Columbus and shopped for all the things we needed for the wedding. Day by day, little by little we got things taken care of. The bridesmaid dresses had to be fitted and ordered.

The cake had to be ordered. The reception had to be planned out. And the party supplies had to be purchased. Jeff decided to hire a friend of his to do the photography. Jeff also had a friend of his to play the organ. I picked my aunt and uncle, Velma and James to sing at my wedding while my cousin Katherine accompanied them at the piano on that big day. Every week I'd go with Jackie to Lazarus in downtown Columbus and try on wedding gowns. Every week I picked a different dress. But I always liked one of the dresses I saw, and it fit every time. It was costly, although it was very beautiful. Every week the price seemed to go down, because no one had bought it. Jackie finally talked our Dad into buying it. It was beautiful and I looked good in it.

Finally, my wedding day had arrived. I awoke in the morning at Jackie and Randy's house. Randy and Jeff spent the night at their brother, Rod's house and took my nephew Jason with them. So, Jackie and I and my niece, Amanda got up that morning. We got dressed and went out for breakfast. After that Jackie took me over to get my hair done. When we got to the First Baptist Church of Granville everything went pretty smoothly. The church was filled with our families and friends. Both of my Grandmothers were there, too. It was a warm autumn day on September 19th, 1987. Jackie was Matron of Honor. My sister-in-law, Georgia was one of my bridesmaids along with three of my cousins who were April Miller and Kathy and Tina Holsinger. My niece, Amanda was the flower girl and my nephew, Jason was the ring bearer. Jeff had a couple of his friends to be ushers along with my uncle Jerry and Randy was an usher, too. The Best Man was Drew McFarland. My Aunt Sharon's husband, Don did a video of the entire wedding and reception.

Jeff and I ate dinner at Mark Pi's China Gate and stayed at the Marriotte Hotel in Columbus. The next morning we got up and ate breakfast at Bob Evan's. It was so neat to be married. We came back to Mom and Dad's house to live there while they both went back to Allentown to live. We were supposed to take good care of their house for them while we stayed there. Dad didn't charge us any rent, but we had to fill the water softener every week and pay for all the utilities. And we had to keep the house and yard neat and clean. Married life was wonderful for the first year. After Jeff lost his construction job, we went through a big problem of trying to manage our money. Jeff got a job at Cellular One, a cell phone company. But, it didn't work out. He was hoping for lots and lots of customers, but no one was buying. So, he quit that job. One time during the winter, there was a job fair in Columbus, and Jeff and I went to it with Jackie and Randy. Another time, Jeff went to a job interview supposedly at IBM in Cincinnati. Even though it sounded like a great job idea that didn't work out either. I thought it would help Jeff get the job if I bought him a pen striped three piece suit, all the more to get the job, right? Jeff said that he met a man downtown in Columbus who was going to take him to the interview and both of them went on the roof of a big building. A helicopter flew them to Port Columbus, so they could transfer to a Lear jet. Jeff said everything was smooth sailing until they got in the office to the job interview at IBM. The job interview began when the interviewer hooked him up to a polygraph machine. One question that Jeff was asked was, "Have you ever had problems with drugs or alcohol in the past?" When Jeff refused to answer that question the job interview ended. Two weeks later Jeff found out that he didn't get that job. It would've been nice and we might have been able to buy a house of our very own. We probably would have been able to do a lot of things, but it just didn't work out that way for both of us. We went out on the town occasionally. Most of the time when we did go out it seemed as if we went to AA Meetings. Sometimes, Jeff's Dad would go to some of the meetings and Jeff and I would see him there. I never did get anything out of those meetings, but I liked to go to them so I could get out of the house. I did not know Jeff was a recovering alcoholic before I married him.

About a year later I wanted to have a baby. I

didn't tell Jeff I stopped taking my birth control pills, I just kept them up on the shelf. Sure enough, I got pregnant around the summertime in 1988. After, I'd awakened with morning sickness we went straight to the hospital and got it checked out. We found out we were going to have a baby in March 1989. Every day I woke up with morning sickness. I was ill the entire eight and a half months of my pregnancy. But, I was so excited about having a little baby and so proud when he came into our lives. Charlie was born on February 24th, 1989. He was a little baby about 6.9 lbs. We had been staying with Jeff's mom Jeannie, and I thought I was in labor the day before. Jeff and I drove to Riverside Hospital. They kept me overnight, because I had borderline toxemia. The doctor induced my labor the next morning and told me I would be in labor for about 14 and ½ hours. We had a little baby boy at 9:45 that night. Jeff and I took turns holding him and just loving on him. He was so tiny. We named him Charles David Ray. I named him Charles after one of my uncles. And Jeff named him David after his middle name.

Jeannie helped me and Jeff take care of Charlie. We had gotten lots of gifts, diapers and clothes, and my parents gave us a play pen and swing. I had a lot of difficulty adjusting to motherhood. I was also seeing a doctor for my mental condition and had to be taken to University

Hospital for postpartum depression. I was there for about 3 weeks. Jeff would drive to the hospital and bring Charlie with him so I could get to see him and hold and feed him. When at last I could finally go home I did much better taking care of him. I was new at being a mother. So, it would take some time to get used to getting up in the middle of the night to warm a bottle. I also had lots of help from Jackie and Georgia.

Later on, my parents asked us if we wanted to move to Allentown and stay with them in their apartment. Dad got Jeff a job at Northeast Jet doing janitorial work. We moved up there and packed all of our clothes, Charlie's baby bed and play pen. It took us all day and part of the night to get there. Charlie was a very good baby. He didn't cry at all during the trip, only when he wanted a bottle. Jeff and I started having marital problems at that time. He would get mad at me for getting up before Charlie woke up. I'd go outside to smoke a cigarette and try to smoke all of it. But Charlie would wake up and he would start to cry for a bottle. This happened a lot of times and I just couldn't seem to get up fast enough before Charlie would wake up. When he did wake up, I was usually downstairs smoking to get prepared for the start of the day. Mom and Dad would get mad at Jeff for yelling at me at the top of his lungs early in the morning. He'd awaken everyone in the whole apartment building. One thing that got on my nerves about Jeff was that he would say he was going to be coming home after work, but he didn't. Sometimes, he decided to stop at a restaurant to eat. I would be mad about it, because I wanted to go with him to the restaurant. He seemed to do this quite a lot in our marriage. I think it was one of my buttons he found to push. Finally, one day my Dad had all he could take. So, he waited until he got in to work one day. Dad asked him to come inside his office for a moment. After Jeff entered the room, Dad closed the door back and locked it. Dad really let him have it, too. He backed him into a corner and laid the law down on him. After that, Jeff went to Dad's boss Earl and he told him that he was resigning. When Jeff came back home he told me he was leaving and going back to Granville to live with his mom. So, we were separated for a while. Then he came back up there and wanted to come back to me and Charlie, and I took him back. But this time he wanted to take me and Charlie and go back to his mom's house to live. I decided to move back to Granville with Jeff and we lived there for about six months or more.

Jeff found a house on the outskirts of Granville on River Road. It was a yellow house with three bedrooms, a big living room and kitchen and dining room, a full bath and full size basement. It needed a lot of work. So, we cleaned it up before we moved in. It had all hardwood floors. There was even a big back yard for Charlie to play in. However, we never went out there, because State Route 16 was at the edge of our backyard.   We had Charlie's first and second birthday party there.   I liked that house, because it was our own house even though we rented it, it was ours. I tried to keep it spruced up, too. I was trying hard all the time to keep a clean house, do the laundry and cook for me and Jeff and Charlie every day. I had my own piano, too, and I would play with Charlie on the piano. I used to put Charlie in his play pen and move it up real close to the piano so he could play on it. One time, Charlie played a couple of notes and then sang the same notes. It was a wonderful little melody. I loved it. I could tell he loved it, too. Jeff had a friend by the name of Dave Walker. He would come to visit us on occasion. Dave gave Jeff a job as editor for a video company. He edited training films. He had a few people working for him including Jeff. Sometimes, Jeff would go to visit other friends of his.

One night, Jeff was out visiting one of his buddies while Charlie and I slept. I woke up in the middle of the night, about two o'clock in the morning. So, I got up, fixed some coffee and lit up a cigarette as I sat in the living room with the lights on. All of a sudden I saw a car drive into my front yard and shine his bright lights through the living room window at me. I got up, made sure the doors were locked and secured and turned off the lights except for a small light in the kitchen. I went into the kitchen and called Jeff at Chuck's house. I told Jeff he better come home now, because there is a guy over here parked in the front yard with his brights on. I told him I was going to call the police. After, I phoned the police they arrived about the same time Jeff did. They both took a flashlight and went out front. The driver apparently had left before the police got there. Sure enough, they both saw tire tracks in the grass where it looked like a car had drove in and turned around to leave.

After the police left, Jeff came back inside the house and called Chuck. He told him that I wasn't lying about it and that there really had been someone who drove in the front yard. I think Chuck might have thought I lied about the whole thing, but that wasn't the case. It had really happened. Jeff came in the living room and asked me if I was ok. Then after we locked the doors, we went to bed. Charlie slept through the whole episode.

12 Saving My Baby's Life

During one afternoon we packed up some laundry and headed to Newark to a laundry mat. It was a cold day in November just a few weeks before Thanksgiving in 1989. As Jeff and I got out of the car, Jeff took the basket full of clothes and headed inside. I got out of the car, got into the back seat to get the stroller in order to fold it out. I put it right outside the car and unbuckled Charlie from the car seat. I'd taken Charlie in my arms, but as I raised my head up and turning toward the stroller to put him in there I lost my balance. I tripped over the stroller. I was in shock about that time and only had a split second to decide what to do. I missed the stroller completely and laid Charlie on the ground ever so gently. Then I forced myself to fall the other way so I wouldn't fall on top of my little baby! I was completely panicked. I knew I didn't want to hurt my baby, so I went the other way on purpose landing on my right shoulder. About that time Jeff came out of the laundry mat. Just then, a man shouted from the other side of the parking lot and asked if he should call for an ambulance. Jeff said not to call the ambulance. Then Jeff said, "Ok, Vickie. Come on. Get up, let's get going."

I said, "But Jeff, I can't get back up." He grabbed Charlie and took him on in the laundry mat. When he came back outside, he said, "Here, let me help you up so we can get the clothes done."

I was in excruciating pain and I was almost in tears. Jeff kept after me to get me to wash the clothes, dry them and get them folded. That night when we got back home I begged Jeff to take me to the hospital. I thought I needed to get my arm looked at. He told me that I could just forget it and told me to stop complaining. The next morning I could hardly get out of bed. I had a hard time getting up. I asked Jeff if he could take me to the hospital that morning, but he said he was going to work. He also told me I needed to use my arm, because all I had wrong with it was just to massage the muscle a while. So, he told me to get in the kitchen and cook his breakfast. I was so upset. Three days went by after that and I just couldn't get any peace. I had to find out about my shoulder and my arm. I called Jeff's boss at the Evergreen's restaurant and talked him into letting Jeff have a couple of hours off so he could take me to the hospital to get my shoulder and arm examined by a doctor. Sure enough Jeff was allowed to come home and take me to the hospital. When Jeff got home he yelled at me real loud asking me why in the world I called his boss to tell him I needed to go to the hospital. I was not only in physical pain, now I was in an emotional uproar. I was so upset and crying. After I was seen by the emergency room doctor, then they took x-rays. I was so impatient I almost decided not to wait around. Finally, the doctor came in the room where Jeff and I were waiting. The doctor said, "It's a good thing you did come in to see us, you have a broken collar bone."

I just stared at Jeff and I didn't say anything. He stared back at me, too. I was so mad at him. I told him that I didn't understand why he refused to take me to the emergency room in the first place. What a terrible experience that was.

I think part of our marital problems could've stemmed from me just not being an adult about everything. As I recall I would get overwhelmed at the drop of a hat. When that happened, I got stressed out. I would make things up and tell Jeff all of these stories that weren't true just to get out of my responsibility. In fact, one time I told Jeff I was hearing voices and I thought I should go to the hospital. I would get stressed out a lot over just little things like taking care of Charlie every day. Making sure that Charlie didn't climb up onto the cabinets, or get into the refrigerator and start pulling things out was a nerve wracking job. It required a lot of patience and steadfastness of my responsibility for my little baby. And I sometimes resorted to making up lies when Jeff came home from work. I'd tell him that I thought I needed to go to the hospital. I said that in hopes that he would take me there so the doctors would admit me, then I'd be free from all of the hardship of looking after our little baby. I feel so awful right now as I'm writing this story, because I was not the mother I should have been to our son. I only hope that Charlie forgives me. I know God has forgiven me and all of my sins. I have forgiven myself and I have a hope now. My hope is in Jesus Christ, the Son of God. I'm so glad to tell you that through it all I managed to help raise our son until he was out of school. Jeff and I separated in 1991 after we had a bad argument.

13 An Unhappy Ending

It happened one evening. I was very tired and I asked Jeff if he would watch Charlie while I went to lie down to take a nap. I just went to bed with my clothes on, because I was so tired and I didn't feel good either. While I was asleep Jeff woke me up and put Charlie to bed with me. Charlie kept trying to get out of bed. While I was having a hard time keeping him in bed with me, Jeff came back into the bedroom and turned on the lights. Jeff walked over to the bed and yelled at me. He told me to get up and put on a nightgown instead of wearing clothes to bed. He also said to get up and clean up the room and put clean sheets on the bed. I couldn't believe he was so unreasonable about all of this. So, I yelled back at him and slapped him, which was something I'd never done to him before. I slapped him a couple of times, too. Then, Jeff told me he was going to call my case manager, Sue and tell her all about this incident. I said, "Ok, go ahead." (I think). Jeff got on the phone and even though it was long after hours, he told them that if my case manager didn't call him back that night he was going to slap a law suit on them and everyone at Mound Builders would be involved. I heard him tell the person on the phone that his wife was a schizophrenic and needed to be locked up. After that, he came back into the bedroom where I was and threatened to tell my case manager to probate me to the state hospital. He might have been really mad at me.

Sue did call back and talked to Jeff for a while, but I didn't hear him say anything about probation. I just went on to bed crying and very upset about the whole ordeal. That night I had a bad dream and when I woke up the next morning, I knew pretty much that our marriage was over. Even though I loved Jeff with all my heart and soul, the painful reality of his rejecting me that much showed me that he never really cared about me as much. The next day I tried to stay out of Jeff's way and stay calm. In the morning, I thought I had a chance to call my parents in Cincinnati. I called them on the phone and told my mother Jeff had threatened to probate me to the state hospital. At that point Jeff came in the room and grabbed the telephone out of my hand and spoke to my mother. Jeff reassured her he was not at all going to do that. He said, we just had a fight and it's over now. But, he didn't say anymore and just hung up the phone. He dared me to call back. Sometime that afternoon Jeff gathered the laundry and said he was going to take Charlie and go to his mom's house and do the laundry for us. Sue called Jeff and talked to him a while. Then, Jeff said that Sue would be over to pick me up to take me in for an appointment with the doctor.

After, Jeff and Charlie left I was there at home by myself. Within about 15 minutes or so, Sue came and I got in her car and we left to go over to Mound Builders in Newark. The doctor asked me all of these questions about what had happened the night before. Then he said you can step out while I talk with Sue for a few minutes. Sue said not to worry that I could just go outside and smoke a cigarette if I wanted. When Sue came outside where I was she said that the doctor told her that he needed to admit me to Grant Hospital in Columbus where they would adjust my medication.

I was in that hospital for about a week. The next day, I called both my parents and told them what had happened and that Jeff managed to put me in the hospital. Then, my parents tried to talk to the doctor who was in charge and she didn't want to talk to them, which made them think this was a bit one sided. They planned a meeting between the doctor, Sue, Jeff and my parents and I. My parents came to the hospital where they went to the meeting room, but the doctor didn't show up for the meeting. Then my parents demanded that they release me from the hospital. So, they did the next day.

14 Moving to Cincinnati

The next morning when my parents arrived, I signed all the necessary paperwork and we all left Columbus. Jeff had told us that he left an envelope inside the mailbox at home that was for me to open. It had some of my money inside of it. When we went over to the house to see Jeff and Charlie, they were not there. I looked inside the mailbox and got the envelope and all that was in there was a check for just seventy-five dollars. He had gotten my social security check, cashed it, and only gave me seventy-five dollars out of my whole check which was over 400 dollars. He did that to me, so I talked about it to my mom and dad and we both agreed that I needed to divorce him. However, Jeff wanted to know where I was staying in Cincinnati, and I would never tell him that. Soon, we made an appointment with a lawyer. The lawyer drew up all the papers for my divorce. Then, we went back home to my mom and dad's apartment in the Spindle Hill Apartments. Meanwhile, my parents had taken me to a social worker who had gotten me started in a clerical training school funded by the Government. I would go to the school downtown about 6 hours per day, 5 days a week. I went through this school for a year and had gotten a lot of training on computers, word processing, data entry, filing, math and English. I didn't receive any pay for the training, but it was somewhere to go to for clerical training. The school had also planned to get me employment after graduation. After graduation I got a job working at the Cincinnati Zoo and Botanical Garden in the Education Office. It was a great job and I was so proud of myself. I found out after getting the job it was only a program designed to prepare me for real employment, which lasted a year until it ended. I was also paid a salary.

One afternoon I picked up the telephone to answer it. It was Jeff so I talked to him a while on the phone in front of my parents. I told him I had gone to a lawyer. Right then he told me to call him back collect. So, I hung up the phone, and told them that Jeff wanted me to call him back collect. I talked my dad into letting me call him back which was a mistake, because then he was able to locate where the call came from so he could send divorce papers to me. My dad called our lawyer and he let us know that Jeff was planning on suing me for gross neglect. It was the biggest mess I'd ever been through in my life.

The day we went to court we had to go up to the Licking County Court of Common Pleas, which was in the middle of downtown Newark. I had to miss a day of school in order to go there to appear in court. First, before we went into the courtroom, my lawyer had taken me aside and said, "If I were you I would take everything that belongs to you from Jeff. Your piano, guitar, bedroom suit, all your clothes and personal things like that I would try to get back. Don't forget anything, Vickie."

I said, "Ok." After the courtroom proceedings were over, Jeff told me he wanted to talk to me outside the courtroom. He looked right at me and said that he never wanted our marriage to end this way, but it had to. Our divorce became final in January 1992. Jeff was given full custody of Charlie. I was only allowed visitation rights. For the next 15 years I would only be allowed to see Charlie sometimes, usually during the holidays and the summertime. I was so grateful for the times that I did get to see him. On the days when I'd see him, we would have a good time together. My mom helped me take care of him most of the time. We worked together as a team in potty training him. And a lot of the time my mom would spend with Charlie while I was in school. I don't know what I would have done without my mom helping me to take care of him. I don't know how Charlie lived with his dad every day while I wasn't with him, but somehow he became a grown man, out of high school and out on his own.

One day I saw an ad in the newspaper about an apartment in Norwood. I called the guy and asked to look at the place. My parents drove me over there and we looked at it. It was in an old house and the house was turned into bedroom apartments. The one I looked at was on the second floor. It had a kitchen and a bedroom with a bathroom off from the bedroom. It had a foldout door for the bathroom. I liked it there and I found a church to go to in Oakley. I called someone about the church and they found a lady that would take me there on Sundays who was Robin. The church I attended was Oakley Square Church of God. And Pastor Chuck Popov was the pastor. I had a very good time going there on Sundays. I also sang in the choir. It was great being a part of a church that really loved me as much as I really loved them, too.

15 An Unhealthy Relationship

I would get up in the morning and get ready to catch a bus to go in to work at the zoo. When I left work I'd catch the bus back into Norwood. And every day I'd usually walk to Empress Chili in back of the Surrey Square Mall. I knew the owners of the place real well. One evening when I walked in to order some iced tea Edie, the manager said there was a man over in the corner booth who wanted to get to know me. I told Edie right away that I really didn't want to go out with anyone, because I belong to a church and sing in the choir. She told me that I could just talk to him for a while and I really didn't have to go out with him anywhere. So, I chuckled a little bit, then paid for my iced tea and walked over to sit down. I sat in the booth right behind the guy Edie was talking about. Finally, he slipped me a piece of paper which said: My name is Otto, and you can call me at this number. I got the note and put it in my purse. When I walked out to go back to my apartment later on that night, I decided I would call him. He made a date with me the next night and I said I'd be there at Hardee's to see him there. I stood him up the next day. He wanted to come over and see me, but I didn't want him to. Later on, I got up and went down to the grocery store and for some reason I'd decided to buy a pack of cigarettes.

I needed more cigarettes after that pack was gone and I knew that man smoked. So, I called him up and asked him if he could take me to the store to get cigarettes. He said, "Sure." After he came inside my bedroom we sat down and talked about my guitar. I played him a song. Right away he said, "I just found a gold mine." I didn't know exactly what he meant by that. But he did say that he was married which I didn't understand. He said he had been separated from his wife long enough to go through the drug and alcohol rehab center at the Salvation Army. I saw him a couple of more times going with him to the Salvation Army Chapel on Sundays. The next couple of days after that I let him stay with me. He stayed with me for three years altogether.

Later, he decided to get out of the Salvation Army in order to move in with me. I couldn't believe I had made such a dramatic change. The pastor's wife called me one morning while Otto and I were asleep. I woke up to answer the phone and it was Billie Jo. I told Billie Jo that I was sorry I hadn't gone to church lately, but I have a boyfriend now who I've been hanging out with at his church at the Salvation Army. She said, "Vickie, having a boyfriend won't make you happy. Being in the will of God will make you happy." I just couldn't understand the seriousness of my life right then with this married man lying next to me. It was adultery.

And it was so hard for me to break that adulterous affair. After three long years of living with him I made him move out off and on. I finally came back to him, but this time I'd gotten pregnant. We were told we had to leave our apartment, too. When that happened he took me over to his son's apartment in Delhi. That was way over on the south side of Cincinnati by about five or six miles out. I stayed there in that little apartment with him. Otto and I slept on the couch in the living room, while his son and his girlfriend slept in the bedroom – a one bedroom apartment. Otto had a job working at the Metropole Apartments downtown as a janitor and painter. He took a bus out there and back. We decided to find another place to live, so we went out to Mt. Washington and found an apartment that was called the El Rancho Rankin Hotel. Otto and I stayed there in that hotel room for about six months. I never liked having to run out of cigarettes. But when I did, I'd bum money from the neighbors so I could keep myself in cigarettes. I would even make drawings with my watercolor pens and drawing paper. I would make use of my time so I could try to solicit people into buying my artwork just so I could buy my cigarettes. Some of the neighbors turned me in. Although, one guy really liked my artwork. I had such a hard time with Otto. He wouldn't give me money so I couldn't buy any cigarettes. He would come home from work and go straight over to the Chinese restaurant and he would drink until way into the night. Sometimes, I would come down to where he worked and we'd go to the bars there, too. I would go with him to four or five bars a night. A lot of times we stayed downtown until late into the night. We would wait for a bus to take us back home. When we finally got back home it was well after midnight. I don't know how we managed not to run into any trouble downtown. We could've been robbed or even killed. But, thank God that never happened.

Finally, one day I'd had all I could take. So, I waited until Otto got to work. I called my parents and told them I wanted to leave Otto for good and not ever go back to him. They both said, "Ok." The day I left him I tried hard not to let on like I was leaving him. But, I waited until he left to go down to the Metropole Apartments and I told my parents they could pick me up and take me back home with them. My dad came that day with his truck and we loaded it up with my clothes and some of my personal things. But, I left a lot of stuff behind. We got out of there before Otto could come back home.

I eventually moved out into an apartment in Amelia, which was a much nicer apartment to live in. I was also seeing a counselor at the Clermont County Counseling Center on a regular basis. We talked a lot about what I would do when my baby came. We also talked about my problem of mismanaging my money.

16 A God Send

One day my mom called me to tell me that my cousin, Julie had called her. She wanted to ask her if it was all right for her to take my baby once he was born and raise him. My mom had told her that it sounded like a great idea and that she was a God send. I told my mom that it sounded like a wonderful idea. Then Julie called me and talked to me for a couple of hours a day. She and I were both very excited about all of this. Later, Julie and her dad and step-mom came down to visit us. Julie had papers for me to sign regarding my decision to let her have him once he was born. So, I signed the papers for her. We also went downtown where Otto worked and had him sign the papers, too.

When I went into labor on the 2nd of January 1995, my parents came to my apartment and had taken me to Anderson Mercy Hospital. My doctor said that my water definitely broke and I told him my plans of giving my baby to my cousin. My sister and brother in-law came down from Newark to be with me and Julie and her parents came to the hospital as well. Julie and her step-mom came into the hospital room where I was hooked up to a monitor and an IV in my arm. We played cards all night it seemed like. My mom was in the room, too. Well, at about 4:00 the next morning it was time for the baby to come. Mom, Anne and Julie came in the room with me to see my baby being born. Anne was on one side of me and my mom was on the other holding onto my hands and guiding me through the breathing methods. We all found out it was a boy. He was exactly 6 pounds. And he was the cutest little baby, just like Charlie was - his older half-brother. After everyone went home the very next day Otto came down to the hospital. But Otto wouldn't give our son his last name. So, I had to use my last name on the birth certificate. While I tried to tell Otto I thought it was a good idea that I give our baby to my cousin, he said it didn't sound like such a good idea to him. He spent the night at the hospital in my room and slept on the fold away bed next to my bed. I had a private room anyway, so it was ok for him to stay there overnight. The next morning Julie and her parents came. I later found out that I was going to be discharged that day. After the doctor came in to check me, he said it was all right for me to go home that afternoon. The social worker of the hospital came in and we talked about what would happen once I left the hospital, where would my baby go and if I really wanted my cousin to have my baby as well. I told the social worker that I wanted my cousin to have my baby and take care of him and that I was giving him to her as a gift. The social worker asked me, "Vickie, are you sure you want these people to have your baby?" With that I replied back to her and said that I did want Julie and her parents to take him. Otto didn't say a word, but I really secretly wanted to keep my baby and raise him myself. The only thing that kept me from doing that was the fact that I was living by myself and I had mental issues. It would be hard for me, especially since I had a smoking problem anyway. I could barely take care of myself. I had a hard time functioning, getting up out of bed every day, doing housework, making sure I had enough food to eat and enough money to live on every month. I had problems also with clinical depression on an ongoing basis.

17 Going Back to Denver to Find Hope

In the spring of 1995 I decided to make a phone call to my old friend, Sylvia who lives in Denver, Colorado. I had called her many, many times and it seemed to be a constant obsession with me. I called directory assistance and found her number. Sure enough I found her phone number and made a call to her. When she answered the phone we talked for hours laughing and talking into the night. I told her I wanted to come back to Colorado and start over again. I wanted to live out there, get a job and an apartment and try to see if her son would like to see me. She said, "Sure, you can come out here and live." I made plans to leave Cincinnati on the 3rd of May that same year. I hadn't thought about how devastated everyone in my family would be. I hadn't really given any thought at all about the hurt that I caused in my family. I thought I was doing the right thing by leaving everything in my apartment in Amelia. I was afraid to tell my parents about going back out to Denver, because I knew they would talk me out of it. I ended up finding out the hard way that you just can't go back and undo what has already been done years ago.

On the morning of the 3rd of May I'd

awakened late. I had packed my suitcase the night before, so I didn't have to do that, all I had to do was get into the shower and then get dressed. After that I called for a taxi cab and told him I wanted to go to the Greater Cincinnati Airport. I also asked him if I could stop by the ATM so I could get money out in order to pay for my airline ticket and the cab fare. He said that was fine. Then we headed down to the airport. When I arrived I got my ticket and checked in my luggage. The attendant who handed my boarding pass to me said I would be making a stop in the O'Hare Airport in Chicago. I would have to change airlines. I was planning on Sylvia and her daughter to be there to pick me up at the airport in Denver. I guess I had some kind of outrageous faith, because I knew she would be there. There was no doubt in my mind about it. Well, when I arrived at the airport and walking down through the corridor, I saw Sylvia and her daughter. They both hugged me and I hugged them, too. We drove back to their house on Lowry AFB. Even though Lowry was a closed base, some of the base housing was available for rent. Outside the airport while she went to go get the car I lit up a cigarette, because I was so anxious and nervous. I hadn't seen my friends in years, 10 years in fact. We walked in their house and I sat down on the couch. Sylvia's daughter said she had to get ready for work. I tried telling both her and her mom that it would be all right to go get some dinner somewhere and I would treat. She said that she couldn't do that, because she had to work the late shift that night and couldn't get the day off.

The next morning after Sylvia let me sleep in her room while she slept on the couch, I'd gotten up late. I hurriedly got dressed and went outside to smoke a cigarette, because I wasn't allowed to smoke in her house. I was thinking about getting together with her son and going out with him, dating him and everything and was planning on getting married to him. The only thing was for sure is that I really wasn't aware that it was over and I could never have been his bride. Not anymore. That would have happened if I met God's timing in 1985. But, it didn't happen, because I left to go back home to Ohio.

When I came back inside to sit down the phone rang. It was a man's voice asking if he could speak to Sylvia. I told him she wasn't here. Then I asked who was calling. And he said, "No."

I said, "Well, ok."

Then, he said, "Goodbye."

And I said, "Goodbye."

Somehow I thought it was him. When Sylvia did come back, I told her about the phone call. She said it might have been her son calling. Sylvia started doing the laundry and I volunteered to help out. Little did I know that's why I was there, to fill in on all the housework that needed done. But I still thought I would get to become Burt's girlfriend soon.

The days went on one by one. Finally, Sylvia took me to her son's house to meet him. He let me borrow his typewriter so I could type my resume. I had plans of getting an office job and I got to use his typewriter. I was nervous about seeing him and gave him a little hug, too. He went downstairs to get the typewriter while Sylvia and I stayed upstairs in the living room. He drove a nice looking Mercedes. He had a big, beautiful house, too. He had some drawings from his little girls posted upon the refrigerator in the kitchen and they were cute. He had a girlfriend who had been living with him, but he kicked her out. She was the mother of his two little girls. We didn't make any plans to see each other. So, we left his house and came back to Sylvia's house.

I talked to Sylvia a lot. She let me know she was not pleased with my behavior. She said I tricked her into thinking I had really grown up as a Christian. We went to church where she and her brother preached. It was a very small church. Some of the members of the congregation had gone there for Sunday services and for Bible Study on Wednesday nights. Sylvia taught Bible Study as well. It shocked me that her nephew who held a position in that church as the music pastor was living with his girlfriend and both of them had children. Yet, Sylvia said I was a sinner, too. I told her I got rid of my boyfriend that I was living with. And this really hurt me. She was blaming me for having gotten pregnant by my boyfriend who had been married even though I went back to God and asked for His forgiveness and then put it all behind me. I told her that. But, she must not have believed me. Some of those people would treat me bad, too. Sylvia also thought I had been making plans to sleep with her daughter's husband. And that just wasn't true. She said when I went outside to go for a walk I was going out there to wait for her daughter's husband to get home so I could coerce him. It seemed that everything was going downhill to the point that she wanted to lock me inside the church for about a week until I learned my lesson. I told her, "You're not really going to do that are you?" She said, "Yes. I am going to do that."

The next few days, I managed to call my parents and tell them where I was and that I was in trouble. My sister was there at the time and she asked me why I'd gone out there in the first place and that I'd left everything in my apartment. Mom and Dad felt sorry for me, but they suggested that I wait until I got my next check and then come on back home.

The next couple of days it seemed as if it was getting worse. We had gone over to a friend's house to visit her. Sylvia decided to go over to see someone else and said I could stay there and visit with that lady for a while longer. Well, Sylvia didn't come back until late into the night. She came back with her nephew, his girlfriend and their little kids. It was now past midnight and we all got into a big, bad argument. It finally ended when I decided to ask if I could call my dad to make arrangements to go back to Ohio tonight. She said I could. She asked her friend if it was all right if I could use her phone to call my dad collect. She said it was ok. So, I called my father and it was now 2:00 in the morning. I woke him up and I asked him if he could let me come back home tonight. Fortunately, he said yes. I was really scared of Sylvia and those people who were tormenting me. They were saying all kinds of things to me to harass me. We left her house and got in the car. Then we came back to Sylvia's house and I packed. Then we got in the car and headed to Denver International Airport, the biggest airport in the world. Anyway, Sylvia, her nephew and I took all of my belongings and sat them on the floor in the airport while I went to talk to the airline attendant. It was now early in the morning about 4:00 I think. Sure enough, the attendant said he'd gotten information from my father who paid for my ticket to Cincinnati, Ohio, but the plane wouldn't be leaving for another 3 or 4 hours. Sylvia and her nephew just left me there in that airport. While they were leaving I said, "Are you going to just leave me here?" And out the doors they went. It was just terrible. I was really crying, too. I was scared. It was a long way from home. It was cold, too, but I had a coat on. I left my luggage and went down to get a sandwich at a shop that was opened and something to drink. Then when I checked my luggage in, I headed down to the waiting area to wait for my flight to arrive. I was so sad and downhearted that I started crying. When I landed at O'Hare Airport and changed airlines I boarded the plane and sat there in my seat crying. One of the stewardess' would ask me periodically if there was something that she could do for me. I couldn't speak. I tried to straighten myself up and it just didn't work. I cried uncontrollably for a long period of time it seemed like. My dad met me at the Greater Cincinnati Airport when I got off the plane in Cincinnati and we talked while he drove us back home. It was heartbreaking to have to face my parents and feel their hurt and anguish. I was wounded badly by the dearest friend I ever had who turned out to be my enemy. I also had to return to the psychiatric unit at Clermont Mercy Hospital. There in that hospital I couldn't get to sleep. The nurse tried several different kinds of medicines, but nothing worked. Finally, the nurse got ahold of the doctor and he prescribed a sleeping pill that would put me right to sleep and it worked. After I had gotten my check I paid my parents back the money it cost them to bring me back home from Denver. I think it was over 500 dollars or more. I don't know if I left some of my things in Denver or not. But I learned a hard lesson. Don't try to go back into your past in order to make things right. Chances are it won't work out in your favor.

18 The Rest of the Story

For the next 15 years I got to see Charlie off and on. We would spend time together when Jeff brought him down to visit. Charlie would stay with his grandparents and me. Jeff would drive down to meet us at a restaurant at the State Route 68 exit at Interest 71, North of Columbus. We would meet them there and Jeff would wait for us there at the restaurant. Charlie would get in the car with us when we pulled up. Then Jeff would go back home. I found out that I couldn't see my youngest son, Jonathan any more. He had a closed adoption, which has caused me a lot of grief and hurt. But, I've finally given it over to God and laid this hurt and pain at the foot of the cross. And God has been faithful to remove all the guilt and condemnation.

In August 1995 I found an apartment that was located in Cincinnati. I was still searching for a church and searching for God. I went to a church nearby. It was a big church called Love and Faith Christian Fellowship. I liked that church a lot. I tried to attend the services every Sunday. I also joined the church choir and really enjoyed it. Later, I found out that Love and Faith Christian Fellowship had a 12 Step program called Alcoholic's Victorious. I decided to go and sit in on those meetings. I quickly made a friend there and she became my sponsor. I had one foot in the church and one foot in the world. I was actually living a compromised Gospel. But I still went to church, because I knew I needed to be there. The thing about it though was that I only wanted God to give me a husband and I didn't know the right channels of finding one. I always managed to find a guy that was not a Christian in my neighborhood. I've never been asked to go on a date by any man from Love and Faith Christian Fellowship. I haven't been dating anyone in a long time for that matter. And I miss dating someone. I miss going out with someone to see a movie and have dinner with.

The reasons why we should have friendship is because you need to share time together with someone you desire to be with. Sharing a laugh with them and encouraging them. And it is telling each other what you would like to do in life. It is talking to each other about your future plans. Friendship is not about meeting someone else's or your own needs. A friend is not someone you confide all your personal secrets to either. Not even a close friend, unless that person is a counselor, a ministry leader or a potential mate. If it is a potential mate, that special someone needs to know all about you. It is part of decision making for marriage. God is our mate, too. The Bible says that He is our husband. We read in Isaiah 54:5, "For thy Maker is thine husband; the Lord of hosts is his name; and thy Redeemer the Holy One of Israel; The God of the whole earth shall he be called." God wants us to come to Him just as we are with all of our faults, mistakes, trials and brokenness. And He wants us to confide in Him everything we have ever done. He desires to have friendship with us. And we need to acknowledge His presence. He knows us inside and out already. And He knows how we will respond to trials and tribulation. He wants to mold us and shape us into His own likeness. He desires to smooth out all the rough edges so He can perfect us into a beautiful diamond someday so that He will be glorified. He is preparing us for our destiny as His Bride. And He is our Bridegroom. He is raising up a mighty army. He needs that closeness with us, just like a husband or a wife needs closeness (intimacy) with each other. Some people get friends to use whatever they can get their hands on. We call those kinds of people users or needy people. And other people have been burned out by friends time after time after time. So, they refuse to have friends. The problem with that is you will isolate yourself from those who love you and who really enjoy your company and friendship.

I met a real handsome man once when I was working part time as a janitor for the Clermont

County Counseling Center. This guy was a Christian. He had the same diagnosis I have, that is Schizophrenia. We both talked a lot about the Bible. He seemed to be a nice Christian man. He invited me a couple of times to his parents' house and one time for Christmas. I had a great time meeting all his brothers and sisters and his nephews and nieces. He was from a very large family. His parents lived in a big house in Milford, Ohio. He lived in the town of Williamsburg. I would go to his house sometimes after work with him. He was a very handsome man and I wanted to marry him. I think I met him when I first started working the part time janitorial job in October 1995. He would come over to my apartment and spend a lot of time with me. We would go out to Denney's or Frisch's sometimes. We mostly sat around my living room talking and playing his CD player. Although, he liked rock music, I would let him listen to it. We both liked to play the guitar and he could play very well. I liked to play his guitar sometimes and we sang, too.

In January 1996 he asked me to marry him. I said, "Yes. I will marry you." I was very happy and on top of the world that night as we both sat together hugging and kissing. We stayed up until the sun came up the very next morning. I went to bed and he laid down on my couch in the living room.

One day we went to his house and were

together all day. I fixed sandwiches and coffee. When he would go to the store to buy food he wanted to go by himself. I tried talking him into letting me go, too, because I wanted to be with him. Well, he had a problem with that. So, he always wanted me to stay there by myself.

We would go to his church on Sunday evenings as well. His brother and sister-in-law attended that church, too. One night he called me and said he didn't want to marry me. But he did say he still wanted to be my friend. Well, I was so upset I couldn't go in to work that night. The following day I got a call from his sister-in-law who told me that he didn't want to marry me, because of all his fears about being married. She said he had problems with relationships and he also had severe problems with anger. After about a year I finally realized I couldn't be married to him that way. His mother had even bought our wedding rings for us. And I wanted to keep my rings. I also had his guitar at my apartment and wouldn't give either of them back. However, my parents said it would be best if I gave him back his rings and his guitar. So, his mother came over one day and I gave her the rings and guitar back, but I was so mad at him for breaking off our engagement. I was very hurt.

I would pray every night before going to bed and I would ask God for a husband. I was so lonely. I thought I needed to be married to someone so I wouldn't be so lonely. It never seemed to happen. The right one hasn't come along yet, if marriage is what God's intentions are for my life.

Now, I am happy living on my own by myself. I have a lot of friends where I live and now I attend Eastgate Community Church.

One day a friend of mine and I decided that we would look for an apartment I could live in that was much safer than the one I was living in. We both knew I needed to move out of there, because it just wasn't a safe environment to live in. There were many people who were moving into that area who had been in prison and who had a history of drug abuse and sex offenders.

She told me she really desired to see me improve by leading me to a much better environment where I would have a safe place to live in. One lady we knew went to our church. She and her boys helped me a lot. So, I decided to move to the same apartment complex. And I've been living here for 6 years. I haven't had any problems at all with my neighbors and every one of them is special to me, including the management. My friend asked permission for the youth leader of our church to move my furniture into my new apartment and every one of the teenage boys from the youth group helped out. What a blessing from God!

I have had a lot of problems in the past with relationships and friendships. I have had a lot of hurt and brokenness in my life. I know what it's like to have been betrayed by a close friend. I know what it's like to lose something valuable and watch it crumble to the ground. I know what it's like to have been in a darkened room where no light is and then many, many years later God comes in and says, "I'm here. I've always been here. I will never, ever, never leave you nor forsake you. I am your way out. Follow me."

One of the things I've learned over the years is that I am careful not to make friendships with people who are angry or people who don't love God enough to live in obedience to Him. I want to live peaceably with all people, especially my family members and friends who are all very dear to me.

I've learned so much over the years in the ways of growing in Christ. Sharing the joys of my heart and learning to help those who are less fortunate than I am are only a few areas in which I've grown. I've also learned how to depend upon the Lord with my finances. Sometimes, I would have difficulty managing my money. But I know God will always help me as long as I depend upon Him. I enjoy making friends with those who love the Lord. One of my best friends lives near me. She has started a women's group to help women cope with life issues. There are almost twenty-five women in the group. I have learned so much from this God-fearing woman. With the Lord's help she has helped me become wiser. She not only has mentored me as a ministry leader, but she has mentored a lot of women in this group as well. And I have watched some of these women grow over the last three years when the group was first started in 2010. I am so thankful she was one of the friends who never gave up on me. And God has never given up on me. He will never give up on any of us as long as we make a home for Him in our hearts and trust Him always.

My hope for you is to wait upon the Lord. Be of good courage, because He has something good in store for all who wait upon Him. The Bible says in Hebrews 11:6, "But without faith it is impossible to please him: for he that cometh to God must believe that he is, and that he is a rewarder of them who diligently seek Him." We also read in Isaiah 40:30-31, [30] "Even the youths shall faint and be weary, and the young men shall utterly fall: [31] But they that wait upon the Lord shall renew their strength; they shall mount up with wings as eagles; they shall run and not be weary; and they shall walk, and not faint."

Also, keep faithful in seeing your doctor and taking the medicine he has prescribed for you. Structure your life and continue to educate yourself as much as possible about your mental health. I also encourage you that if you don't already have a personal relationship with Jesus Christ to invite him in your heart right now. Just say this prayer out loud, "Dear Lord God, I am a sinner. I have done many things in my life that I am not proud of. I know I need to change my life. I cannot do this on my own, but I ask you now to come into my heart and set me free. I ask for your forgiveness of all my sins throughout my whole life. Please forgive me of every one of them. I know Father that Jesus Christ is your only Begotten Son. I know, too, that Jesus Christ, your only Begotten Son died on the cross to save me from your wrath to come. I also know that Jesus Christ, the Son of God was raised from the dead and is alive forever more. He is seated on your right hand in your Throne in Heaven. Help me to live a life that is worthy of your grace and love. I ask you now to give me a new life. I praise you Father, because I know you can change me and give me hope. I trust you this day as I commit my life to you. I thank you for accepting me just the way I am. I thank you for my new life in Christ. I am a new creature. The old has passed away. And the new has just begun. I pray this prayer in Jesus' Name, Amen." If you have said that prayer, go to a good Bible based church and fellowship there. Find a Bible Study to attend. Keep reading and studying your Bible. Pray often and tell others about your new life in Christ.

I am so thankful to be alive today and to be able to share my story with those who need encouragement, and those who suffer from mental illness. I praise God and I thank Him for helping me through the valleys I walked through all by myself. I thank Him for helping me to come out of the darkness into His marvelous light. And through it all I am still praising Him today!

To God be the glory! Amen.

www.ingramcontent.com/pod-product-compliance
Lightning Source LLC
Chambersburg PA
CBHW070552290526
45790CB00002B/654